Bowmar/Noble Handwriting E

Reviewers

Sister Andrew Maureen, I. H. M.
Principal
Somerdale, New Jersey

Dr. Fred Chavez
Specialist, Elementary Reading
Los Angeles, California

Beverly Ellis
Elementary Language Arts Supervisor
Springfield, Missouri

Otis H. Lovelace, Jr.
Principal
Charlotte County, Virginia

Dr. Philip Mann
Professor of Psychology
University of Miami, Florida

Dr. Virginia S. Melton
College of Education
Louisiana Tech University, Louisiana

Jeannie Russell
Instructional Specialist
Rosemead, California

Sister Kathleen T. Sullivan
District Superintendent
Staten Island, New York

Mary Janet Taylor
Director of Elementary Instruction
Blytheville, Arkansas

Sister Mary Theiss
Curriculum Coordinator
Milwaukee, Wisconsin

McGraw-Hill School Division
1200 Northwest 63rd Street
Oklahoma City, Oklahoma 73116-5712

Cover Illustration: Mike Wimmer
Illustrations: Murray McKeehan

ISBN 0-07-375765-9
ISBN 0-8372-4056-5

44 LKV 25

PRE-TEST

Some panthers walk in dim jungles, and some wolves live in quiet city zoos. Zoo bears and pandas exercise quite often. Red foxes get their exercise by jumping high fences.

B H E F J M
O Q P G V X

1 2 3 4 5 6 7 8 9 10

Directions: Copy the paragraph, letters, and numerals.

CURSIVE ALPHABET

Models of all the cursive letters and numerals are presented on this page.

Aa Bb Cc Dd Ee

Ff Gg Hh Ii Jj

Kk Ll Mm Nn Oo

Pp Qq Rr Ss Tt

Uu Vv Ww Xx Yy Zz

1 2 3 4 5 6 7 8 9 10

Directions: Copy the letters and numerals.

SMALL LETTERS

The upper-loop small letters are **e, l, h, k, b,** and **f.** They begin with a curve up from the baseline. All upper-loop small letters, except small **e,** curve up almost to the top line.

e e eeee every evening

Please let me explain.

l l llll lovely hill

The ladder was left outside.

h h h hhhhh healthy higher

Beth hit a home run.

Directions: Copy the letters, words, and sentences.

1 2 3 k k k k kkkkk knocked kicked

The kettle is in the kitchen.

1 2 b b b bbbbb baseball babies

Bobby has a blue umbrella.

1 2 f f f fffff fifty officers

Jeff fell off the fence.

Directions: Copy the letters, words, and sentences.

SMALL LETTERS

The oval small letters are **o, c, a, d, g,** and **q.** Above the baseline, both small **g** and small **q** are the same as small **a.**

o o o ooooo one o'clock

His book is not open.

c c c ccccc color chicken

You can exercise with the music.

a a a aaaaa against apart

The parade will start at noon.

 Directions: Copy the letters, words, and sentences.

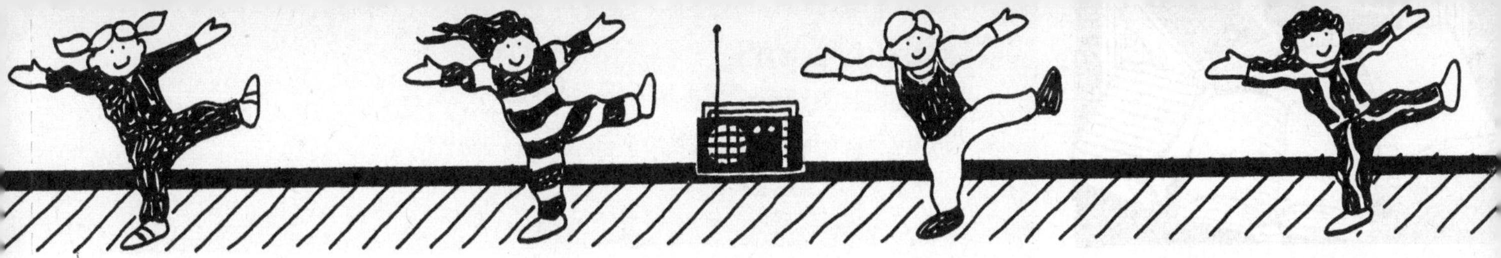

d d d ddddd didn't dry

The dark road was muddy.

g g g ggggg going ragged

We all began to giggle.

q q q q qqqqq quite quaint

Our quilt is quite warm.

Directions: Copy the letters, words, and sentences.

CONNECTIVES

Connectives join letters together to form words. They also set the spacing between the letters in words.

Under-curve connectives

little tie test rush

kettle meet neither cup

Listen carefully to the instructions.

Over-curve connectives

any tag sand many

daddy end ago in

Explain the example to Larry.

Directions: Copy the words and sentences.

Long under-curve and long over-curve connectives

glass jet jump just

gas game zone zoo

Did you just begin your studying?

Connectives from the baseline

far press fresh paper

proper question quality

The fifth part is quite difficult.

Directions: Copy the words and sentences.

IMPROVING HANDWRITING: SIZE

Checking your letters for size will help you to improve your handwriting. Straight lines drawn with a ruler should just touch the tops of your letters.

All capital letters are almost a full space high.

Election Day is in November.

The letters **b, f, h, k,** and **l** curve up almost to the top line.

He always thinks before he speaks.

The letters **d, p,** and **t** are two-thirds of a space high.

Did you watch the parade yesterday?

All the other small letters are one-third of a space high.

Everyone could answer the question.

Directions: Copy the sentences. Use a ruler as you check for size.

IMPROVING HANDWRITING: SLANT

Checking your letters for slant will help you to improve your handwriting. Dashed lines drawn through the downstrokes of your letters should be parallel and slanted.

The capital letter downstrokes are slanted and parallel.

Is New Mexico near New York?

Part of the small letter downstroke is a straight, slanted line.

All that glitters is not gold.

The slanted downstrokes should be slanted in the same direction.

Why didn't Ricardo try again?

The Handwriting Guide Sheet can be used to check slant.

Wealth can't buy health.

Directions: Copy the sentences. Use a ruler as you check for slant.

USING HANDWRITING: PARAGRAPH

The first line of a paragraph is always indented with a space as wide as a capital **O.** The hyphens in this paragraph divide words that do not fit on the line.

Every six months Diego visits
the dentist. He tries to do every-
thing the dentist tells him.
Diego brushes and flosses his
teeth every day. Brushing
cleans the surface of his teeth.
Flossing cleans the spaces be-
tween his teeth. Diego always
eats balanced meals to keep
his teeth and his whole body
healthy.

Directions: Copy the paragraph.

USING HANDWRITING: POEM

The colon in this poem is used before the statement of a rule. The colon is made with two dots, one above the other.

Learn to Spell

If you want me to read your work,
This rule remember well:
You have to write your letters right
And also learn to spell.

The trouble with my spelling, yes,
(I've known it all my days)
The same old sound is often spelled
In several different ways.

Directions: Copy the poem.

IMPROVING HANDWRITING: WATCH-OUT LETTERS

When small **a, b, d, e, h,** and **o** are not carefully formed, they may look like other letters.

Keep the oval in small **a** closed at the top.

a a a aaaaa aaaaa aaaaa

Keep the end stroke of small **b** close to the guideline.

b b b bbbbb bbbbb bbbbb

Keep the oval of small **d** closed at the stem.

d d d ddddd ddddd ddddd

bead date black

Would you erase the chalkboard?

 Directions: Copy the letters, words, and sentence.

Keep the loop in small **e** open.

e e eeeee eeeee eeeee

Keep the hill of small **h** well rounded.

h h h hhhhh hhhhh hhhhh

Keep the end stroke of small **o** close to the guideline.

o o o ooooo ooooo ooooo

hotel opera rough

Choose your favorite house.

Directions: Copy the letters, words, and sentence.

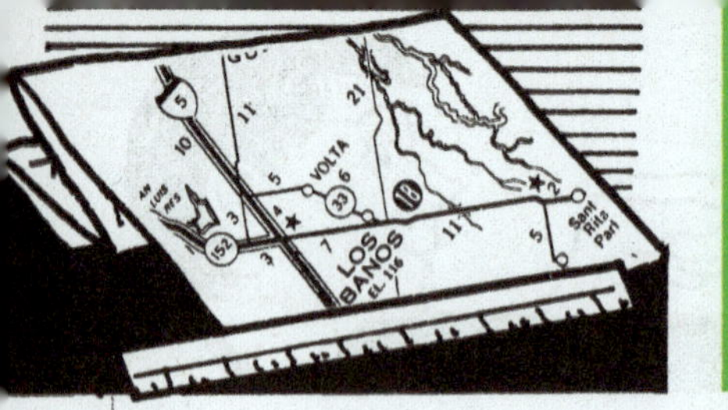

USING HANDWRITING: COMPOSITION

The title of this composition is centered on the first line with a blank below.

Planning a Trip

Linda looked carefully at a
California map. Her family was
planning to drive from Los
Angeles to San Francisco, and she
was helping to plan the trip.
What was the shortest route?
Linda wanted to find out how
many miles her family would
have to drive.
Linda located Los Angeles and
San Francisco on a map. She
found a highway that connected
them: Interstate 5. She measured
the distance with a ruler: five
inches. On the scale of miles,
one inch was equal to 75 miles.
She had all the information
she needed:
Route: Interstate 5
Distance: 375 miles

Directions: Copy the composition.

101

PROGRESS PAGES

lead held deaf

ahead check hello

deck leak cheek

dad cage half

cab lake lab

ache each add

Directions: Copy the words.

glad glee age

edge eagle ago

egg gale go

equal fall face

fell quack fled

fade flee fill

Directions: Copy the words.

MANUSCRIPT ALPHABET

Manuscript writing is useful in preparing posters, labels, signs, greeting cards, and charts.

Aa Bb Cc Dd Ee Ff

Gg Hh Ii Jj Kk Ll

Mm Nn Oo Pp Qq Rr

Ss Tt Uu Vv Ww Xx

Yy Zz

1 2 3 4 5 6 7 8 9 10

Be kind to animals. Safety First.

Cross the street when the light is green.

Directions: Copy the letters, numerals, and sentences.

USING HANDWRITING: FORMS

Manuscript writing is often used to fill out forms.

Name: Wilson, John Thomas
LAST FIRST MIDDLE

Address: 531 Monroe Avenue
NUMBER AND STREET

Chicago, Illinois 60611
CITY STATE ZIP CODE

Telephone Number: 141-7728

Date of Birth: June 24, 19--
MONTH DAY YEAR

Age: 10 Grade: 4

School: Monroe Township School

Teacher: Miss Mary Josephson

Name: ______________________________
LAST FIRST MIDDLE

Address: ______________________________
NUMBER AND STREET

____
CITY STATE ZIP CODE

Telephone Number: ______________

Date of Birth: ______________________
MONTH DAY YEAR

Age: ____________ Grade: ____________

School: ______________________________

Teacher: ______________________________

Directions: Copy the form. Fill in a year.

SMALL LETTERS

The pointed small letters are **i, j, u, w, t, p, r,** and **s.** The tops of these letters are closed and pointed. The points of small **r** and small **s** rise a little above the guideline.

1 2 dot i i iiiii inside invite

1 2 dot j j jjjjj juice enjoy

Juan just invited Kim to join us.

1 2 3 u uuuuu uncle turn

1 2 3 4 w wwwww will would

The sun shone through the wide window.

Directions: Copy the letters, words, and sentences.

1 2 across t t ttttt title little

1 2 3 p p ppppp pepper poppy

Carmen put too much pepper on the potatoes.

1 2 3 r r rrrrr river roar

1 2 3 s s sssss lesson season

Chris rode on the silver train.

Directions: Copy the letters, words, and sentences.

SMALL LETTERS

The small letters that have hills and valleys are **m, n, v, x, y,** and **z.** These letters curve up in a rounded hill and slant down to the baseline.

m m m m mmmmmm my moment

The museum opened last summer.

n n n nnnnn none tunnel

Kenji has nine green pencils.

v v v vvvvv very love

The village lies in a valley.

Directions: Copy the letters, words, and sentences.

slant across

x x xxxxx except exit

I will fix six extra lunches.

y y yyyyy yes yearly

A cat played with the yarn.

z z zzzzz zero zipper

A dozen bulldozers moved the dirt.

Directions: Copy the letters, words, and sentences.

BRIDGE CONNECTIVES

Bridge connectives join small **b, o, v,** and **w** with letters that begin at the guideline.

oats away lodge clock

boast vacuum bake variety

The wood is in the back room.

van roam wasp board

log zoo bank wait

We watched the boat at the dock.

 Directions: Copy the words and sentences.

HORIZONTAL CONNECTIVES

Horizontal connectives join small **b, o, v,** and **w** with letters that begin at the baseline.

went better dove very

poem even well between

The potatoes were very hot.

wrap cover built violet

orange bubble opera vest

Don went to see the western movie.

Directions: Copy the words and sentences.

USING HANDWRITING: COMPOSITION

In a composition, the first line of each paragraph is indented. The title is centered on the first line with a blank line below.

Honeybees

Maybe you think that honeybees are insects that only buzz and sting. They are much more interesting than that! If you looked into a hive, you would see one bee that is larger than the rest. This is the queen, whose only job is to lay eggs. Worker bees have much more to do.

Young workers clean the wax rooms that hold the baby bees. Older workers leave the hive to gather pollen and nectar. Pollen is used for food, and nectar is used for making honey. A returning worker tells other bees where nectar can be found. The worker performs a strange, whirling dance. The dance tells the other bees where to look!

Directions: Copy the composition.

IMPROVING HANDWRITING: SHAPE

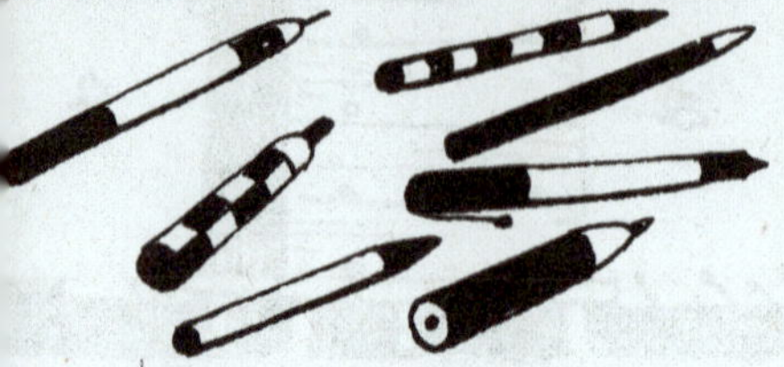

Checking your letters for shape by comparing them to correctly formed models will help you to improve your handwriting.

The ovals in **a, d, g, q,** and **o** should be closed at the top.

The squirrel gathered many acorns.

The tops of **i, j, u, w, t, p, r, d,** and **s** should be pointed.

We waited until the rain stopped.

The loops of **b, e, f, h, k,** and **l** should be open.

Look both ways before crossing.

The hills and valleys of **m, n, v, y,** and **x** should be well rounded.

Have you finished every exercise?

Directions: Copy the sentences and check your handwriting for shape.

IMPROVING HANDWRITING: SPACING WORDS

Checking the spacing between words will help you to improve your handwriting. The space between words should be as wide as a small **o.**

Japan's capital is Tokyo.

Japan has many islands.

Monsoons affect Japan's climate.

Japan grows soybeans.

Japan has a large fishing industry.

Japan has had many earthquakes.

Directions: Copy the sentences. Use a ruler as you check for spacing.

USING HANDWRITING: BOOK REPORT

In a book report, the title and author of the book are usually written at the top of the first page. The title of a book is always underlined.

The Courage of Sarah Noble
by Alice Dalgliesh

This book tells the true story of Sarah Noble, a young girl who lived in colonial times. In 1707, when she was only eight years old, Sarah had a great adventure. She left her mother and her brothers and sisters and went with her father to Connecticut. There in the wilderness, she lived in a cave while her father built a house.

In Connecticut Sarah was often lonely and scared, but she remembered what her mother had told her, "Keep up your courage, Sarah Noble. Keep up your courage."

Sarah learned an exciting new way of life. She learned the customs and ideas of her new Indian friends. Sarah did keep up her courage. She began to love her new home.

 Directions: Copy the book report.

IMPROVING HANDWRITING: WATCH-OUT LETTERS

When small **i, t, r, m,** and **n** are not carefully formed, they may look like other letters.

Keep the top of small **i** pointed. Remember to dot the letter.

i i i i iiiii iiiii iiiii

Keep the stem in small **t** closed. Remember to cross the letter.

t t t t ttttt ttttt ttttt

Keep the top of small **r** pointed.

r r r r rrrrr rrrrr rrrrr

trick right rabbit

The little train is very dirty.

Directions: Copy the letters, words, and sentences.

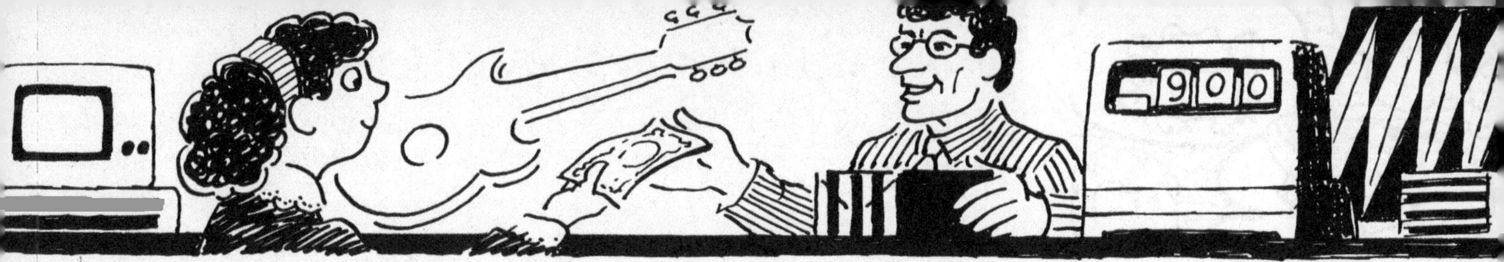

Keep the three hills in small **m** well rounded.

m m m m mmmmm mmmmm

Keep the two hills in small **n** well rounded.

n n n nnnnnn nnnnnn nnnnnn

monkey thimble snow

The amount was nine dollars.

This sentence contains all the watch-out letters.

The train was bound for home.

Directions: Copy the letters, words, and sentences.

USING HANDWRITING: PARAGRAPH

Sets of quotation marks are used in this paragraph to show the exact words of a speaker. Quotation marks are written just under the top line.

Animal Languages

People who speak different languages describe animal sounds in different ways. People who speak English describe the sounds that frogs make as "ribbit, ribbit." People who speak Spanish describe the same sounds as "croa, croa." In English, a bird says, "cheep, cheep," while in Spanish, a bird says "pio, pio."

 Directions: Copy the paragraph.

USING HANDWRITING: PARAGRAPHS

Sets of quotation marks are used in this paragraph around a short title or name. Quotation marks are shaped like commas.

America—"Land of Opportunity"

America has been a "Land of Opportunity" since the days of the first settlers. Millions of people have come here to start a new life. They have brought with them new languages and new ideas. Working together, they have all helped to make the United States a great nation.

Directions: Copy the paragraph.

PROGRESS PAGES

twin	swim	zoom
wax	visit	write
join	your	win
zoo	box	wave
with	money	own
wren	wife	wet

Directions: Copy the words.

stop very fox

buzz better bridge

form room log

move orange spoon

proud knock cover

coat cloud doll

Directions: Copy the words.

USING HANDWRITING: PARAGRAPHS

In these paragraphs, hyphens are used between the two parts of compound words. In both manuscript and cursive writing, the hyphen is made just below the guideline.

The World of Ballet

Dancers rise on the tips of their toes and spin like tops. They leap up high and float slowly through the air. Welcome to the world of ballet.

Ballet dancers are graceful dancers. They are also well-conditioned athletes They can control their bodies to make difficult movements look easy. As they sway to the music, they bring joy-filled moments to those who watch them.

Directions: Copy the paragraphs using manuscript handwriting.

USING HANDWRITING: NUMBERED LIST

A numeral with a period is written before each item in a numbered list.

Important Dates in American History

1. America was discovered in 1492.
2. Jamestown was settled in 1607.
3. The Pilgrims arrived in 1620.
4. The colonists declared their independence from Great Britain in 1775.
5. The United States became a new and independent nation in 1783.
6. The Constitution became the law of the new nation in 1788.

Directions: Copy the list using manuscript handwriting.

CAPITAL LETTERS

Capital **A, O,** and **C** are the oval-shaped capital letters. Capital **O, C, D,** and **E** all have loops. Capital **P, R,** and **B** all begin with a slanted stroke.

The first stroke of capital **A** goes around to the left.

A A A Arthur August

Capital **O** ends near the top line.

O O O Oliver Oregon

Capital **C** begins with a loop. Then it curves left.

C C C California Carlos

Capital **E** has a horizontal loop midway in the space.

E E E E England Eugene

 Directions: Copy the letters and words.

Capital **D** has a small loop at the baseline.

D D D Dan Dorothy

The downstroke of capital **P** is slanted.

P P Paula Peter

The second stroke of capital **R** slants back up.

R R Rick Ruth

Capital **B** has a small loop above the guideline.

B B B Betty Bill

Directions: Copy the letters and words.

CAPITAL LETTERS

Capital **F, T, S, G,** and **I** all have boat endings like capital **B.** Capital **J** loops below the baseline. Capital **L** and **Q** curve below the baseline.

Capital **F** begins with a reverse curve.

F F F February

The end stroke of capital **T** should be kept low.

T T Twan Tennessee

The upper loop of capital **S** is crossed at the guideline.

S S S Sumi Spain

The upper loop of capital **G** is half the size of **G.**

G G G Geneva Gale

Directions: Copy the letters and words.

Capital **I** begins at the baseline.

I I I Indiana Idaho

The upper loop of capital **J** is twice as wide as the lower loop.

J J John Japan

The end stroke of capital **L** curves below the baseline.

L L L Larry London

The end stroke of capital **Q** is like the one in capital **L**.

Q Q Q Quentin Queen

Directions: Copy the letters and words.

USING HANDWRITING: MATH PROBLEMS

In math problems, the numerals are often lined up in columns or rows.

$$\begin{array}{r} 23 \\ +45 \\ \hline 68 \end{array} \qquad \begin{array}{r} 67 \\ +89 \\ \hline 156 \end{array} \qquad \begin{array}{r} 96 \\ -54 \\ \hline 42 \end{array} \qquad \begin{array}{r} 32 \\ -21 \\ \hline \end{array} \qquad \begin{array}{r} 64 \\ -10 \\ \hline \end{array}$$

$$\begin{array}{r} 3 \\ \times 6 \\ \hline 18 \end{array} \qquad \begin{array}{r} 5 \\ \times 2 \\ \hline 10 \end{array} \qquad \begin{array}{r} 7 \\ \times 4 \\ \hline 28 \end{array} \qquad \begin{array}{r} 8 \\ \times 2 \\ \hline \end{array} \qquad \begin{array}{r} 9 \\ \times 1 \\ \hline \end{array}$$

$4+3=7 \qquad 5+5=10 \qquad 9-2=$

$3 \times 2=6 \qquad 5 \times 1=5 \qquad 6 \div 2=$

Directions: Copy and solve the problems.

USING HANDWRITING: MATH PROBLEMS

The symbol $ is written before a numeral and means **dollars.**

Seven minus two equals five. 7-2=

Three plus six equals nine. 3+6=

Four times two equals eight. 4X2=

Ten divided by two equals five. 10÷2=

Mrs. Tagawa bought 8 glasses. Each glass cost $4.00. How much did 8 glasses cost? 8X4=32 They cost $__________.

Directions: Copy and solve the problems.

IMPROVING HANDWRITING: ALIGNMENT

Checking the alignment of your letters will help you to improve your handwriting. All your letters should sit on a straight line drawn through the bases of your letters.

We have all learned the lesson.

The judge spoke quietly to the jury.

Locate Quebec on the map.

Jamaica is in the West Indies.

The katydid is a green insect.

Bad beginnings make bad endings.

Directions: Copy the sentences. Use a ruler as you check for alignment.

IMPROVING HANDWRITING: OVERALL APPEARANCE

Checking the overall appearance of your written work will help you to improve your handwriting. A paper should have even margins and neat handwriting.

(Use your name.) (Use today's date.)

Skip a line.

The Big Dipper

Skip a line.

The Big Dipper is the name of
a group of seven stars seen in the
northern sky. These seven stars
are called the Big Dipper because
they form the outline of a long-
handled cup. The two stars that
form the front of the cup point
to the North Star.

Directions: Copy the paragraph. Check the overall appearance of your paper.

USING HANDWRITING: POEM

Each line of this poem begins with a capital letter. Every other line is indented.

February Twilight

I stood beside a hill
    Smooth with new-laid snow,
A single star looked out
    From the cold evening glow.

There was no other creature
    That saw what I could see—
I stood and watched the evening star
    As long as it watched me.

—Sara Teasdale

Directions: Copy the poem using cursive handwriting.

USING HANDWRITING: PARAGRAPH

In this paragraph, the title begins on the left side of the page.

The Erie Canal

The Erie Canal was the first important national waterway built in the United States. The canal was completed in 1825. By joining the Great Lakes with the Atlantic Ocean, the canal provided a valuable route for the shipment of goods between the East and the West.

Directions: Copy the paragraph.

IMPROVING HANDWRITING: WATCH-OUT NUMERALS

Be careful: **5**'s can look like **3**'s
6's can look like **0**'s
7's can look like **1**'s

Start the last stroke of **5** where you began the numeral.

5 5 5 55555 55555 55555

Keep the loop in **6** between the guideline and the baseline.

6 6 66666 66666 66666

Keep the down stroke of **7** straight and slanted to the left.

7 7 7 77777 77777 77777

Mr. Wu read 576 pages last week.

Eric was born on April 5, 1976.

 Directions: Copy the numerals and sentences.

USING HANDWRITING: PARAGRAPH

This paragraph contains the watch-out numerals: **5, 6,** and **7.**

Pony express riders began carrying mail in 1860. They rode between Missouri and California. The express stations were 10 to 15 miles apart. Riders went swiftly between the stations, changing to a fresh horse at each stop. Each rider rode about 75 miles, then turned the mail over to another. The service ended in 1861.

Directions: Copy the paragraph.

USING HANDWRITING: TABLE

Each important word in a title or name is capitalized. Every month begins with a capital letter.

Do You Know These Holidays?

Bunker Hill Day	June 17
Colorado Day	August 2
Bennington Battle Day	August 16
Admission Day	September 9
Child Health Day	October 5
Will Rogers Day	November 4
Wyoming Day	December 10
Bill of Rights Day	December 15
Forefather's Day	December 21

Directions: Copy the table.

USING HANDWRITING: MATH PROBLEMS

When the symbol ¢ follows a numeral, it means **cents.**

The world's first Ferris wheel was displayed at the Chicago World's Fair in 1893. It cost 50 cents to ride the Ferris wheel 2 times. How much did it cost to ride it once?

50÷2=25 It cost ____¢.

Another popular ride was a long moving sidewalk. It cost 5 cents to ride it once. How much did it cost to ride 5 times?

5X5=25 It cost ____¢.

Directions: Copy and solve the problems.

PROGRESS PAGES

John Quincy Adams was born
in 1767.

In 1933, Franklin Delano Roosevelt
became President.

Oregon became a state while
James Buchanan was President.

Grover Cleveland dedicated the
Statue of Liberty in 1886.

 Directions: Copy the sentences.

The new President in 1953 was Dwight Eisenhower.

Franklin Pierce was elected President in 1852.

Abraham Lincoln was born on February 12, 1809.

Theodore Roosevelt became President at the age of 42.

Directions: Copy the sentences.

USING HANDWRITING: POSTER

In this poster, each line is centered. The first word in each line is capitalized and each important word in the title is capitalized.

Kinds of Food We Should Eat Daily

Meat, fish, chicken, or eggs

Leafy green and yellow vegetables

Milk, cheese, or yogurt

Bread or cereals

Oranges, orange juice, and other fruit

Directions: Copy the poster using manuscript handwriting.

USING HANDWRITING: FORMS

Application forms often ask for a signature. Signatures are usually written in cursive handwriting.

TO BE FILLED IN BY APPLICANT

LAST NAME ANDERSON

FIRST NAME JAMES

MIDDLE INIT. R

ADDRESS 12849 WRIGHT ST

CITY OAK PARK STATE IL

ZIP CODE 60540

AREA CODE 312 9809238

I WISH TO BORROW LIBRARY MATERIALS FROM THE PUBLIC LIBRARY. I WILL OBSERVE ALL RULES ESTABLISHED BY THE LIBRARY, AND WILL BE RESPONSIBLE FOR ALL MATERIALS BORROWED ON MY CARD, WITH OR WITHOUT MY CONSENT. I ALSO AGREE TO PAY ANY FINES OR OTHER CHARGES IMPOSED FOR LATE RETURN OR MUTILATION OF LIBRARY MATERIALS.

SIGNATURE *James R. Anderson*
-TO BE SIGNED IN PERSON BY APPLICANT

TO BE FILLED IN BY APPLICANT

LAST NAME

FIRST NAME

MIDDLE INIT.

ADDRESS

CITY STATE

ZIP CODE

AREA CODE PHONE

I WISH TO BORROW LIBRARY MATERIALS FROM THE PUBLIC LIBRARY. I WILL OBSERVE ALL RULES ESTABLISHED BY THE LIBRARY, AND WILL BE RESPONSIBLE FOR ALL MATERIALS BORROWED ON MY CARD, WITH OR WITHOUT MY CONSENT. I ALSO AGREE TO PAY ANY FINES OR OTHER CHARGES IMPOSED FOR LATE RETURN OR MUTILATION OF LIBRARY MATERIALS.

SIGNATURE ______________________
TO BE SIGNED IN PERSON BY APPLICANT

Directions: Copy the form.

CAPITAL LETTERS

Capital **H, K, M, N, V, U,** and **Y** all have cane beginnings.

The downstrokes of capital **H** are slanted and parallel.

H H Helen Harry

The small loop in capital **K** should touch the beginning stroke.

K K Karen Kent

The second hill in capital **M** is shorter than the first hill.

M M Maine Mary

Capital **N** is like capital **M** with one less hill.

N N Ned November

Directions: Copy the letters and words.

Capital **V** ends at almost the same height as the first stroke.

V V Virginia Venus

Capital **U** begins like capital **V.**

V U U Utah Uranus

Above the base line, capital **Y** is like capital **U.**

V Y Y Yukon Yankees

Sentences and names always begin with capital letters.

Yes, Venus and Uranus are planets.

Directions: Copy the letters, words, and sentence.

CAPITAL LETTERS

Capital **W, X,** and **Z** all begin with small loops and downward curves.

Capital **W** is pointed at the top and at the baseline.

W W W W Washington

The first stroke of capital **X** begins and ends with a loop.

X X X Xavier X ray

The second loop in capital **Z** touches the baseline.

Z Z Zola Zachary

All capital letters should be the same height.

Zeb visited Wales and Xochimilco.

Directions: Copy the letters, words, and sentence.

USING HANDWRITING: PARAGRAPH

The first line in a paragraph is indented. The paragraphs about Switzerland contain all the letters of the alphabet.

Switzerland

Switzerland is one of the loveliest countries in Europe. It is also the most mountainous. Many tourists go there to enjoy the beauty of its quiet lakes and to ski in the snowy Alps.

Switzerland is famous throughout the world for its excellent clocks and watches. Among its principal cities are Geneva, Bern, and Lucerne.

Directions: Copy the paragraphs.

WRITING RHYTHMICALLY

Writing rhythmically will help you to write faster and more smoothly and easily.

1 1 1 1 1 1 1 1 1 1

e e e e e eeeee

1-2 1-2 1-2 1-2 1-2 1-2 1-2 1-2 1-2 1-2

a a a a a aaaaa

1-2 1-2 1-2 1-2 1-2 1-2 1-2 1-2 1-2

n n n n n no no

1-2 1-2 1-2 1-2 1-2 1-2-3 1-2 1-2-3 1-2

o o o o o so so

1-2 1-2 1-2 1-2 1-2 1-2 1-2 1-2 1-2 1-2 1-2

v v v v v van van

1-2 1-2 1-2 1-2 1-2 1-2 1-2 1-2 1-2 1-2 1-2-3 1

c c c c c can came

Directions: Copy the letters and words as you count the strokes.

1-2 dot i 1-2 dot i 1-2 dot i 1-2 dot i 1-2 dot i 1-2 1-2 . 1-2-3 dot air 1-2 1-2 . 1-2-3 dot air

1-2-3 m 1-2-3 m 1-2-3 m 1-2-3 m 1-2-3 m 1-2-3 1-2 1-2-3 1-2 mama

1-2-3 r 1-2-3 r 1-2-3 r 1-2-3 r 1-2-3 r 1-2-3 1-2 1-2 ran 1-2-3 1-2 1-2 ran

1-2-3 s 1-2-3 s 1-2-3 s 1-2-3 s 1-2-3 s 1-2-3 1 1 see 1-2-3 1 1 see

1-2-3 u 1-2-3 u 1-2-3 u 1-2-3 u 1-2-3 u 1-2-3 1-2-3 1 use 1-2-3 1-2-3 1 use

1-2-3-4 w 1-2-3-4 w 1-2-3-4 w 1-2-3-4 w 1-2-3-4 w 1-2-3 1-2 1-2-3-4 saw 1-2-3- 1-2 1-2-3-4 saw

Directions: Copy the letters and words as you count the strokes.

USING HANDWRITING: INVITATION

In this invitation, the heading, closing, and signature all begin in the middle of the line.

Heading { 19 Travis Drive
Akron, Ohio 44302
April 11, 19__

Dear Fred, } Greeting

I am having a party Saturday, April 21, from 5 to 7. All your friends will be here. We can play games and have lots of fun. Can you come?

Closing { Your friend,

Signature { Harry Jones

Directions: Copy the invitation. Fill in the year in the heading.

USING HANDWRITING: ADDRESSING AN ENVELOPE

The name and address of the person receiving the letter are written in the center of the envelope. The sender's name and address are written in the upper left corner.

Harry Jones
19 Travis Drive
Akron, Ohio 44302

Mr. Fred Smith
721 Lamar Street
Akron, Ohio 44302

Directions: Copy the addresses.

REVIEW

The ovals in small **a, d,** and **o** should be closed at the top.

a a a   already   anyway

aboard   again   alarm

d d d   dropped   dried

daydream   deed   depend

o o o   outdoors   o'clock

onion   odor   opposite

Directions: Copy the letters and words.

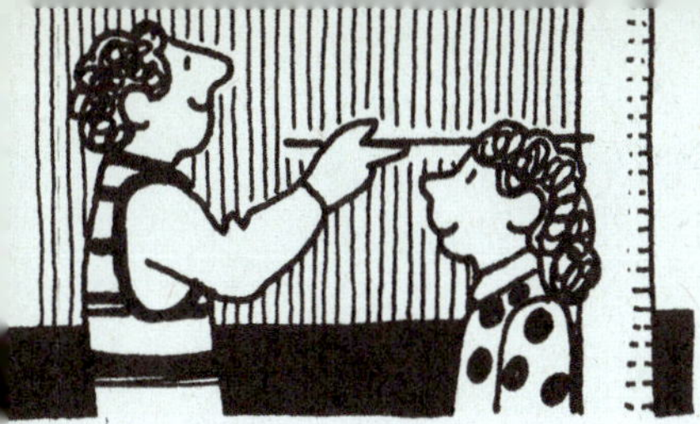

REVIEW

The hills in small **h, m,** and **n** should be well rounded.

h h h healthy higher

height hush headlight

m m m mean mind

mom member mumble

n n n named number

nine none nation

Directions: Copy the letters and words.

REVIEW

The loops in small **e, l,** and **b** should always be open.

e e e electric either

every eaten elephant

l l l lovely little

lonely level lively

b b b baseball bubbles

baby bulb blackboard

Directions: Copy the letters and words.

REVIEW

The tops of small **i, t,** and **d** should always be closed.

i i i invited interest

inside insist imagine

d d d did dressed

decide drive dotted

t t t thought that

teeth taste truth

Directions: Copy the letters and words.

USING HANDWRITING: NUMBERED LIST

The numerals in this list are lined up one under the other.

Tips on Bicycle Safety

1. Obey all traffic signs and traffic laws.
2. Use hand signals to stop and turn.
3. Keep to the right when riding in the street.
4. Ride in single file.
5. Walk across busy street crossings.
6. Keep bicycle parts clean and oiled.
7. Make sure the tires have enough air.
8. Never carry a second rider on a bicycle built for one person.

Directions: Copy the list using cursive handwriting.

USING HANDWRITING: PARAGRAPH

The first line of a paragraph is always indented with a space as wide as a capital **O.**

The United States of America

In one nation, the United States combines the arctic snows of Alaska and the tropic islands of Hawaii. It includes green farmlands and glaring deserts. Its tall mountains reach to the sky, and its plains stretch out wide and flat. Americans are proud of their amazing country!

Directions: Copy the paragraph.

PROGRESS PAGES

Wouldn't it be exciting to travel the great waterways of the world? Imagine boating for hundreds of miles along the Ural, the Mississippi, the Yukon, and the Zambesi Rivers. Think of floating peacefully down the Kennebec or the Nile. Wouldn't you like to cross Lake Huron and Lake Victoria, and see the floating gardens of Lake Xochimilco?

Directions: Copy the paragraph.

Writers have been working at their art for thousands of years. Homer and Xenophon were writers in ancient Greece. Voltaire and Zola were famous French writers in later centuries. William Butler Yeats, MacKinlay Kantor, Sigrid Undset, and Mary Norton are some famous modern authors.

Directions: Copy the paragraph.

USING HANDWRITING: COMPOSITION

Developing a smooth rhythm while you write a composition will help you to increase the speed of your handwriting.

Wilma Rudolph

At age four, Wilma Rudolph could not walk because of a serious illness. At age six, she could walk just a little. Does this sound like the early life of a gold-medal Olympic champion? Wilma's family helped her to overcome her problem. She learned to walk and then run.

Later, Wilma was able to play basketball. In high school she was on a track team. She ran so well that she made the 1956 Olympic team. During the 1960 Olympics, she won three gold medals. She was so strong and graceful that she was called "The Gazelle." The little girl who could not walk became one of the world's finest athletes.

Directions: Copy the composition.

FINAL TEST

As the sun rises and moves across the United States, people begin to wake up. They get up in Queens, New York, and Roanoke, Virginia, and in East Liverpool and Xenia, Ohio. The sun moves west to Villa Park and Zion, Illinois, and to Great Bend, Kansas. Dawn comes to Dallas, Texas, to Jackson Hole, Wyoming, and Albuquerque, New Mexico. Morning comes to Flagstaff, Arizona, Ventura, California, and Honolulu, Hawaii.

Directions: Copy the paragraph.

HANDWRITING GUIDE SHEET

The Handwriting Guide Sheet is placed under your writing paper. It is used to check letters for correct slant and to check for uniform spacing between words.